Animal Young

Birds

Rod Theodorou

Heinemann
LIBRARY

First published in Great Britain by
Heinemann Library,
Halley Court, Jordan Hill, Oxford OX2 8EJ
a division of Reed Educational and Professional
Publishing Ltd.
Heinemann is a registered trademark of Reed
Educational & Professional Publishing Ltd.

OXFORD MELBOURNE AUCKLAND
JOHANNESBURG BLANTYRE GABORONE
IBADAN PORTSMOUTH (NH) USA CHICAGO

Designed by Celia Floyd
Illustrations by Alan Fraser
Printed in Hong Kong/China

03 02 01 00 99
10 9 8 7 6 5 4 3 2 1

ISBN 0 431 03078 2

British Library Cataloguing in Publication Data

Theodorou, Rod
  Birds. – (Animal young)
  1. Birds – Infancy – Juvenile literature
  I. Title
  598.1'39

Acknowledgements

The Publishers would like to thank the following for
permission to reproduce photographs:

BBC: Michael & Patricia Fogden p. 8, Pete Oxford p.
10, Yuri Shibnev p. 16, Warwick Sloss p. 23; Bruce
Coleman: John Cancalosi p. 5, Pacific Stock p. 6, Jen
& Des Bartlett p. 9, Kim Taylor p. 14, George
McCarthy p. 17; NHPA: Gerald Lacz p. 7, Pierre Petit
p. 19, E A Janes p. 24; OSF: Martyn Chillmaid p. 11,
Ben Osborne p. 15, Ian West p. 18, Kathie Atkinson
p. 22, Stan Osolonski pp. 25, 27; Planet Earth: Allan
Parker p. 20, Julian Hector p. 26; Tony Stone: Rene
Sheret p. 12, Art Wolfe p. 13, John Warden p. 21.

Cover photograph reproduced with permission of
Oxford Scientific Films/Robert A Lubeck

Every effort has been made to contact copyright
holders of any material reproduced in this book.
Any omissions will be rectified in subsequent
printings if notice is given to the Publisher.

Any words appearing in the text in bold, **like this**,
are explained in the Glossary.

Contents

Introduction

There are many different kinds of animals. All animals have babies. They look after their babies in different ways.

These are the six main animal groups.

Mammal

Bird

Reptile

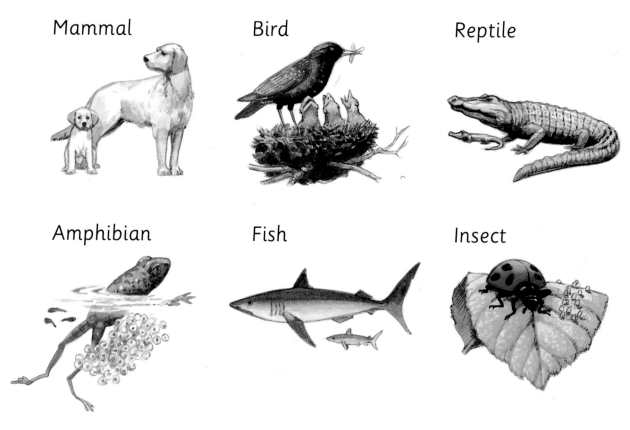

Amphibian

Fish

Insect

This book is about birds. Birds live all over the world. They all lay eggs. Baby birds **hatch** from the eggs. The babies are called chicks.

These are mute swan chicks.

What is a bird?

All birds:
- have two wings
- have feathers
- have a **beak**
- **lay** eggs.

Bald eagle

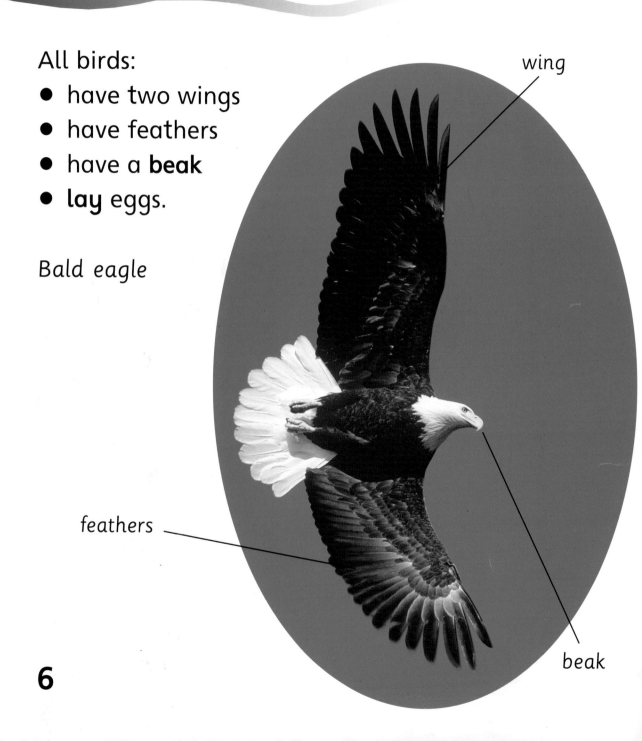

wing

feathers

beak

Most birds:

- can fly
- make a nest to lay their eggs in.

Penguins are birds that cannot fly. They use their wings to help them swim.

Making a nest

Most birds build nests. They build them with things they can easily find, like grass, twigs and mud. The nest will keep their eggs warm and safe from **enemies**.

This tiny hummingbird nest is made from cobwebs, leaves and **moss**.

Some birds dig holes into the earth to make their nests. Woodpeckers peck holes in trees or **cacti** to live in. Sometimes other birds nest in old woodpecker nests.

This elf owl is nesting inside an old woodpecker hole in a cactus.

Eggs

Some birds can **lay** over 15 eggs every year. Inside every egg is a growing chick. The egg is full of yellow **yolk** that feeds the chick.

The giant albatross lays only one egg every two years.

Most birds sit on their eggs to keep them warm until they **hatch**. The chick breaks open the eggshell using a sharp bump on its **beak**. This bump is called the 'egg tooth'.

A new chick is called a **hatchling**.

Hatchlings

Some **hatchlings** are born blind and helpless.
They are small and weak and have no feathers.
Their parents have to feed them every day.

These blind sparrow hatchlings open their
mouths to be fed when they hear their parents.

Other kinds of chicks are born with their eyes open and covered with soft feathers. They can run about to find their own food.

These ostrich chicks leave the nest and follow their parents soon after **hatching**.

Feeding the hatchlings

Parent birds have to find food and bring it back to the hungry **hatchlings** all day long. Many birds lay eggs in the summer, because there is more food to eat.

This bluetit has to catch over 400 caterpillars every day to feed its chicks!

Some **seabirds** fly out to sea to catch and eat fish. When they fly back to their nest they bring this food back up into their **beaks** for their chicks.

This albatross chick is feeding from its parent's beak.

15

Life in the nest

Sometimes the bigger chicks eat all the food. The smallest chick may die from hunger, or even be pushed out of the nest by the bigger chicks.

This golden eagle chick may have killed its brothers and sisters.

Cuckoos lay one egg in another bird's nest. When the cuckoo chick **hatches** it pushes the other eggs out of the nest. The other birds think it is their own chick.

This poor reed warbler is feeding a huge cuckoo chick.

Learning to fly

Soon the chicks are ready to learn to fly. They hold onto a twig and flap their wings a lot to practice and make them strong.

Pheasant chicks are ready to fly only two weeks after **hatching**.

Some parent birds help their young to learn to fly. They fly away from the nest and call to their chicks. The chick may get food as a **reward**.

This harrier chick is learning to fly.

Finding food

This young starling is old enough to catch its own food.

Even when they can fly, many chicks stay close to their parents. They may **beg** for food. But the parents stop feeding the chicks to make them find their own food.

Some chicks can feed themselves, but their mother shows them the best places to find food. First she calls to her chicks. They run to her and follow her.

Ducklings always follow their mother in a line.

Staying safe

There are many animals, like foxes, which eat young birds. Some chicks have the same colour feathers as the place they live. This helps them hide away from **enemies**.

These plover chicks look like pebbles.

Seabird chicks have no trees or grass to hide in. Their parents live in huge groups, called colonies, so they can help each other fight off enemies.

Hundreds of gannets live in this nesting colony.

Looking after the young

If an **enemy** comes close to a place where birds are nesting, it may get mobbed by all the parents. This means the parents fly very close to it, even pecking at it.

These crows will mob this heron until it flies away.

Some birds **protect** their chicks by **pretending** to fly badly, as if they had a broken wing. A hunter will often follow the parent, leaving the chicks safe.

This killdeer is pretending it is hurt.

Growing up

Some chicks grow up very fast. Some are fully grown in only 20 days from hatching. Larger birds may take up to a year to become an adult.

This albatross chick's soft **down moults** so adult feathers can grow.

Once the chicks are fully grown they do not stay with their parents. They may live in bigger groups called flocks. Some **migrate** huge distances every year.

These migrating young geese fly behind the older females.

		Fish
What they look like:	Bones inside body	all
	Number of legs	none
	Hair on body	none
	Scaly skin	most
	Wings	none
	Feathers	none
Where they live:	Lives on land	none
	Lives in water	all
How they are born:	Grows babies inside body	some
	Lays eggs	most
How they feed young:	Feeds baby milk	none
	Bring babies food	none

Amphibians	Insects	Reptiles	Birds	Mammals
all	none	all	all	all
4 or none	6	4 or none	2	2 or 4
none	all	none	none	all
none	none	all	none	few
none	most	none	all	some
none	none	none	all	none
most	most	most	all	most
some	some	some	none	some
few	some	some	none	most
most	most	most	all	few
none	none	none	none	all
none	none	none	most	most

Glossary

beak   the hard, pointed part of a bird's mouth

beg   to ask for something very strongly

cacti   (one = cactus) plants with no leaves that grow in deserts

down   small, soft, fluffy feathers that cover a chick's body and keep it warm

enemy   an animal that will kill another animal for food or for its home

hatch   to be born from an egg

hatchling   name for a baby when it has just been born from an egg

lay   when an egg comes out of a female bird's body

migrate   to move from one place to another each year

moss   small, soft, green plant which grows on soil, wood or stone

moult   when chicks lose their old feathers and grow new adult ones

pretend   do something that is not real

protect   to look after

reward   to be given something for being good or doing something well

seabird   birds that live near the sea and get their food from it

yolk   part of an egg that is food for a baby animal

Further reading

Bat and Bird, Rod Theodorou and Carole Telford, *Spot the Difference*, Heinemann Library, 1996.

Birds, Philip Steele, *Pocket Facts*, Macmillan, 1990.

Birds, Rob Hume, *Tracker Nature Guides*, Hamlyn, 1991.

Bird Facts, *Nature Facts and Lists*, Usborne, 1990.

Heavy and Light, Rod Theodorou, *Animal Opposites*, Heinemann Library, 1996.

The Dorling Kindersley Big Book of Knowledge, Dorling Kindersley, 1994.

The Usborne Book of World Wildlife, Usborne, 1994.

What is a bird?, Robert Snedden, Oxford Scientific Films, Belitha Press, 1992.

Index